Lerner SPORTS

ALL-STAR SMACKDOWN

CRISTIANO RONALDO VS. DIEGO MARADONA

WHO WOULD WIN?

ANNE E. HILL

Lerner Publications ◆ Minneapolis

For Elsi Bakken, my favorite soccer star—and Ronaldo's biggest fan

Lerner Publications Company
An imprint of Lerner Publishing Group, Inc.
241 First Avenue North
Minneapolis, MN 55401 USA

For reading levels and more information, look up this title at www.lernerbooks.com.

Main body text set in Aptifer Sans LT Pro. Typeface provided by Linotype AG.

Editor: Nicole Berglund **Photo Editor:** Nicole Berglund **Lerner team:** Sue Marquis

Library of Congress Cataloging-in-Publication Data

Names: Hill, Anne E., 1974– author.
Title: Cristiano Ronaldo vs. Diego Maradona : who would win? / Anne E. Hill.
Other titles: Cristiano Ronaldo versus Diego Maradona
Description: Minneapolis, MN : Lerner Publications, [2025] | Series: All-star smackdown | Includes bibliographical references and index. | Audience: Ages 7–11 | Audience: Grades 2–3 | Summary: "Playing pro soccer decades apart, Cristiano Ronaldo and Diego Maradona have both dominated the field. But who is the true king of soccer? Readers can compare their careers and choose the winner"— Provided by publisher.
Identifiers: LCCN 2024009017 (print) | LCCN 2024009018 (ebook) | ISBN 9798765648230 (library binding) | ISBN 9798765661390 (paperback) | ISBN 9798765653111 (epub)
Subjects: LCSH: Ronaldo, Cristiano, 1985-—Juvenile literature. | Maradona, Diego, 1960–2020—Juvenile literature. | Soccer players—Portugal—Biography—Juvenile literature. | Soccer players—Argentina—Biography—Juvenile literature.
Classification: LCC GV942.7.R626 H55 2025 (print) | LCC GV942.7.R626 (ebook) | DDC 796.334092 [B]—dc23/eng/20240307

LC record available at https://lccn.loc.gov/2024009017
LC ebook record available at https://lccn.loc.gov/2024009018

Manufactured in the United States of America
2-1012791-53381-5/1/2026

TABLE OF CONTENTS

Diego Maradona

INTRODUCTION

LEGENDS ON THE FIELD

Diego Maradona's first FIFA World Cup in 1982 was disappointing. Team Argentina had failed to make the semifinals. But in 1986, he was ready to fight. Maradona and Argentina needed a win against

Fast Facts

- Diego Maradona played with the Argentina national team in the 1982, 1986, 1990, and 1994 World Cups. They won in 1986.
- Maradona won the FIFA Player of the Century award in 2000.
- Cristiano Ronaldo has won both the Golden Ball and FIFA's Player of the Year five times.
- Through 2023, Ronaldo has played in 1,200 professional games and scored 868 goals.

England to advance to the semifinals. Maradona made an exciting goal that he accidentally scored with his hand. It became one of the most famous goals in World Cup history.

But it was his next goal that really wowed the world. Maradona took the ball in the middle of the field. With great skill, he ran past five English players to score. His goal took his team to the semifinals against Belgium. Argentina beat Belgium and went on to beat West Germany for the championship. Maradona was voted the best player of the tournament and received the Golden Ball award.

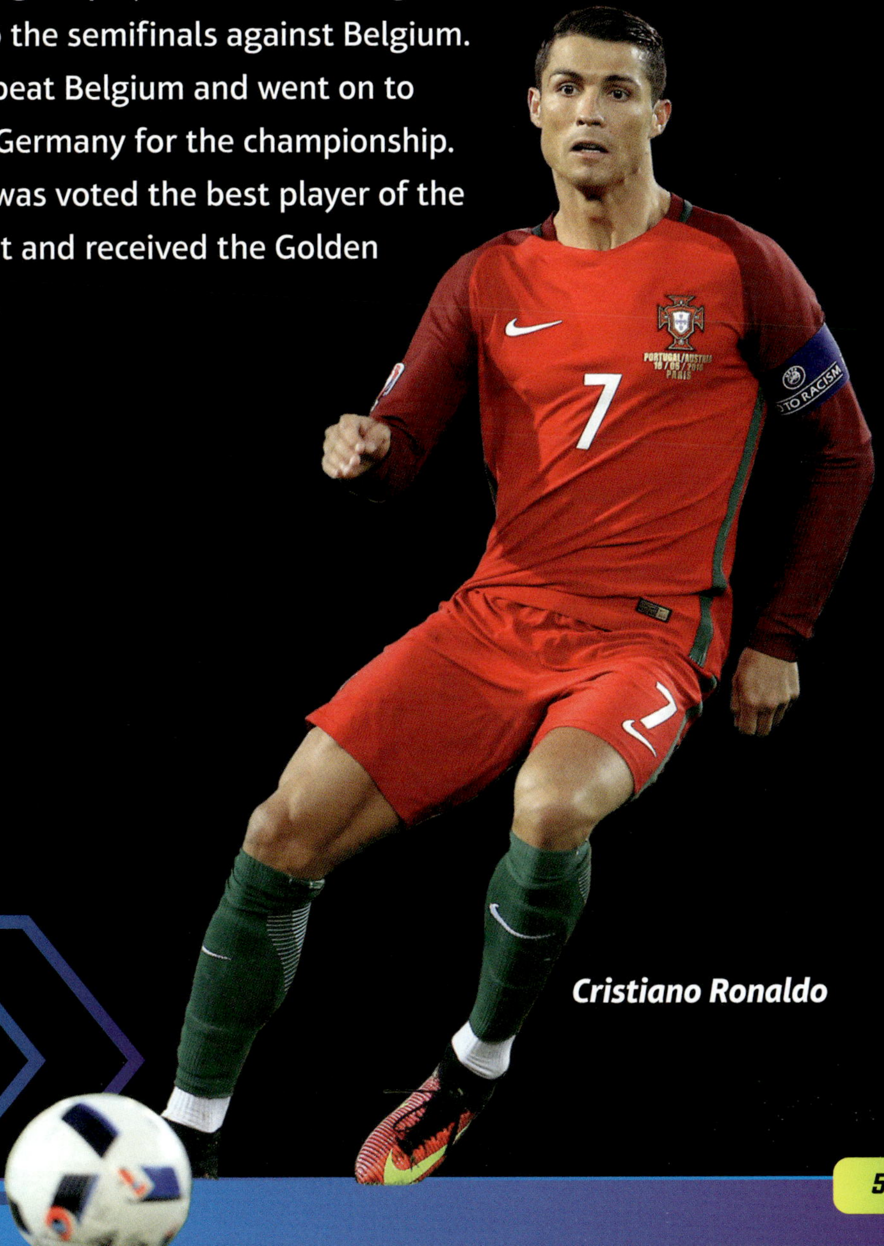

Cristiano Ronaldo

Cristiano Ronaldo has yet to win a World Cup. But he has shattered records in the sport. As Team Portugal's captain, he has made his country proud. In 2016, Portugal competed in the European Championship. Ronaldo led his team with three goals and three assists in the tournament. He helped Portugal beat France to win the title.

Maradona and Ronaldo are among the best soccer players in history. But which player will win this smackdown? Keep reading to decide!

Ronaldo holds the trophy after winning the 2016 European Championship.

Maradona celebrates after winning the 1986 FIFA World Cup.

CHAPTER 1

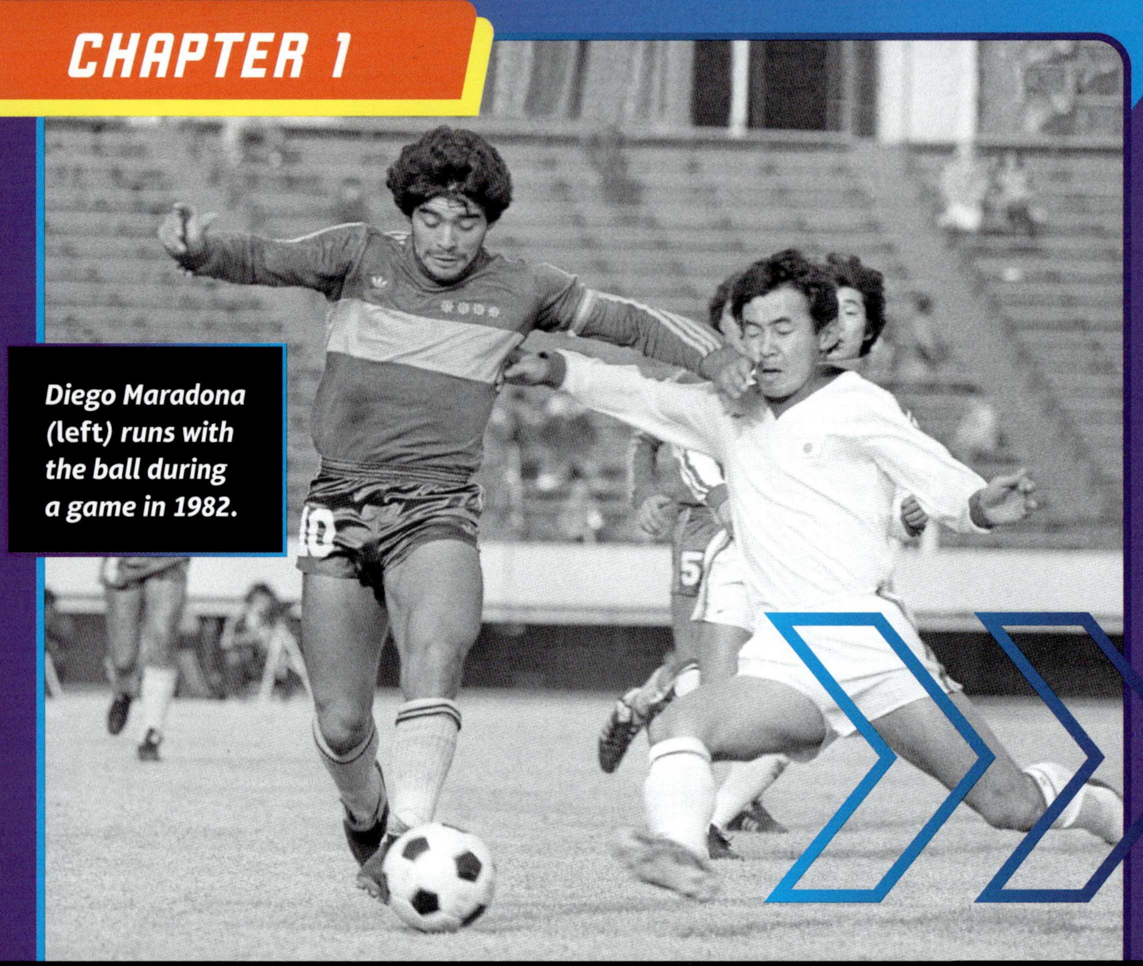

Diego Maradona (left) runs with the ball during a game in 1982.

HUMBLE BEGINNINGS

Diego Armando Maradona was born on October 30, 1960, in a town just outside of Buenos Aires, Argentina. Diego's family had little money. He had seven siblings. When he was three years old, a family member gave him a soccer ball. Diego loved the ball and was hardly ever seen without it.

His soccer talents led him to try out for a junior team at eight years old. The coaches could not believe he was so young and talented. They even asked for proof of his age. Diego didn't make the junior team, so he joined a boys' team called Las Cebollitas, or the Little Onions. With Diego on the team, they won 136 games in a row.

Diego (left) *plays for the Argentinos Juniors in 1980.*

Diego continued to improve his skills. During halftimes at senior team games, he performed tricks with soccer balls. At 15, he became the youngest person to ever play for the Argentinos Juniors. He scored 116 goals in his five years on the junior team.

Diego warms up for a match with Barcelona in 1982.

Maradona (right) chases the ball during a 1984 Barcelona game.

Barcelona is a pro soccer team in Spain. They brought Maradona to their top team in 1982. He quickly became known as a fast player with a strong temper. As an attacking midfielder, he was responsible for passing the ball and defending. Many fans were drawn to his style of play. Even fans of other teams could tell that Maradona was a special player. After Barcelona, Maradona played for other teams in Europe.

CONSIDER THIS

Before he signed his first big contract with Manchester United, Ronaldo learned that he had a heart condition that required surgery. He only stopped playing briefly and made a full recovery.

Cristiano Ronaldo dos Santos Aveiro was born on February 5, 1985, in Madeira, Portugal. He is the youngest of four children. Cristiano's family did not have much money. He discovered soccer through his dad, who worked at a local soccer club. Cristiano loved the sport. He even practiced soccer at night when he was supposed to be home in bed.

Ronaldo celebrates during a 2001 game with Manchester United.

Ronaldo (right) fights for the ball during a game in 2004.

At 18, Ronaldo signed with Manchester United as a forward. The team paid about $15 million for Ronaldo to join the team, making him the most expensive teenage player at the time. Ronaldo quickly proved he was worth the money. His footwork and skill on the pitch led to multiple league championships. In 2008, Ronaldo was named FIFA World Player of the Year.

CHAPTER 2

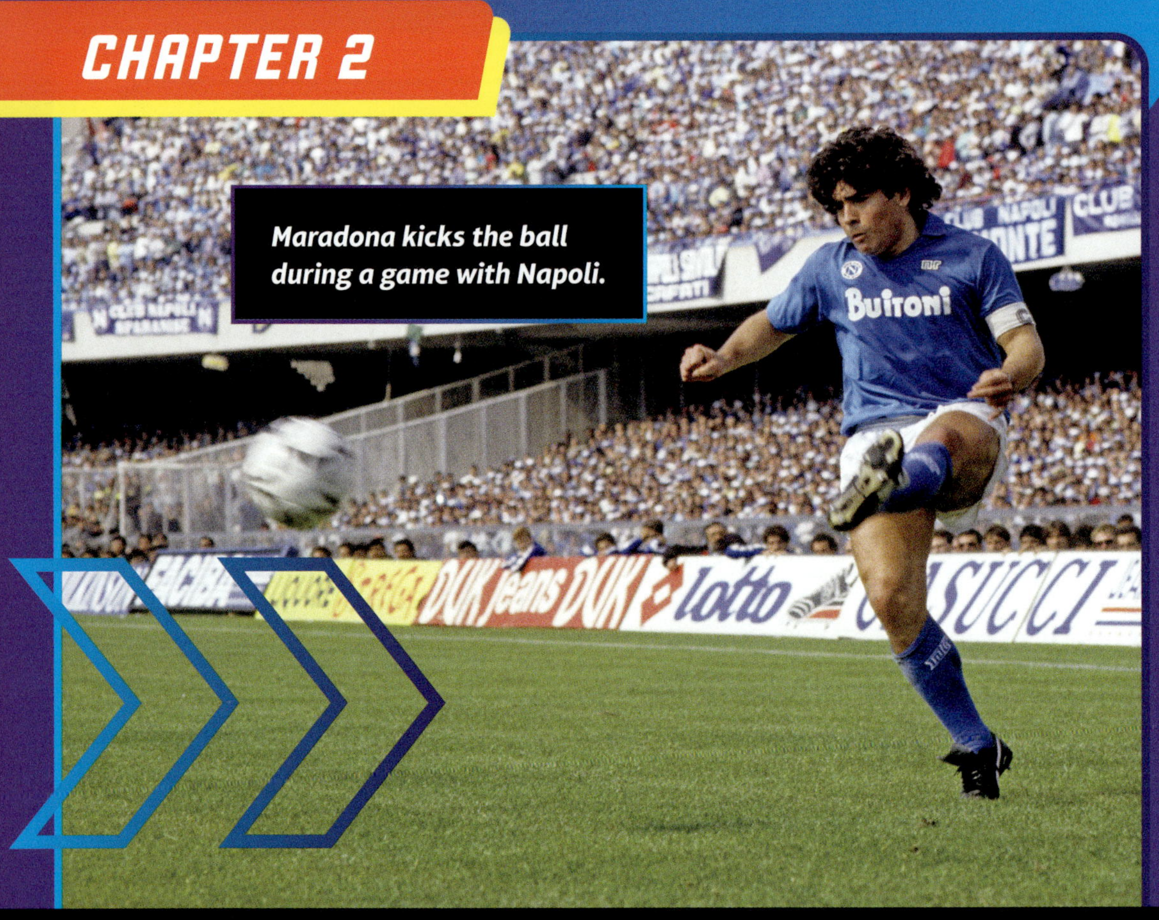

Maradona kicks the ball during a game with Napoli.

BIG MOMENTS

Maradona was one of the best soccer players of the 1980s. He is also seen by many as the greatest of any era. He was awarded the FIFA Player of the Century award in 2000. The award has only been given once. Maradona shared the honor with another soccer legend, Pelé. The award was the highlight of Maradona's career.

Maradona was very famous in Argentina. People loved his control over the ball, especially after his 1986 World Cup win. But he was also adored by soccer fans around the world. He played for seven years in Naples, Italy, for SSC Napoli. Before Maradona's arrival in Naples, the team was not strong. But that soon changed. He led Napoli to their first country title in 1987, as well as their second in 1990.

Maradona celebrates after Napoli won the country title in 1987.

Maradona (left) plays for Napoli in 1988.

In 2002, the Argentine Football Association requested that FIFA retire Maradona's famous number 10. When a number is retired, it honors the player. No other player can wear that number in the league. The request was denied. But many think that no other player should wear that number.

CONSIDER THIS

The Argentinos Juniors soccer team named their stadium after Maradona. Ronaldo has also been honored by his country. A bronze statue of Ronaldo is at the airport in his hometown of Madeira.

Maradona celebrates his induction into the Italian Football Hall of Fame.

Soccer is called football in most places outside of the US. In 2005, Maradona was inducted into the Italian Football Hall of Fame. He also entered the International Football Hall of Champions that year.

Ronaldo has set records playing for Manchester United, Real Madrid, and Juventus. With Manchester, he set scoring records and earned FIFA's Player of the Year award. He led Real Madrid to a European Championship and FIFA Club World Cup. With Juventus, Ronaldo led his team to an Italy Cup.

Playing for Real Madrid, Ronaldo (front left) heads the ball during a 2012 game.

Ronaldo holds his Golden Ball award in 2008.

Ronaldo is the highest-paid pro soccer player of all time. In 2023, he made $136 million. But Ronaldo has more than just money. He is the pride of Portugal and the national team captain. He has won the Golden Ball award five times. He was also named FIFA's Player of the Year five times. In January 2024, he even received an award named after Maradona. Ronaldo won the Maradona Award for Best Goalscorer after he scored 54 goals in 2023.

CHAPTER 3

Maradona (left) runs after the ball in the 1990 World Cup.

LEGACIES

Both Maradona and Ronaldo have been the stars of their teams. Maradona played for the Argentinos Juniors from 1976 to 1981. After joining FC Barcelona in 1982, he helped them win the 1983 Spanish Cup.

Maradona joined SSC Napoli in 1984. He led the team to league titles in 1987 and 1990. His shining moment as a player was the 1986 World Cup. No one could deny his talent as a player.

Maradona (left) plays for Napoli in 1990.

CONSIDER THIS

Maradona retired from playing pro soccer in 1997. In 2008, he became head coach of the Argentina national team. The team made it to the 2010 World Cup. He also coached several other clubs until 2018.

Ronaldo plays for Juventus in the 2019 European Championship.

Ronaldo has been a force in soccer since he began playing. In 2004, he led Manchester United to the Football Association Challenge Cup. Ronaldo left Real Madrid for the Italian club Juventus in 2018. The winning streak continued. He helped Juventus win two league titles. In 2021, Ronaldo briefly went back to Manchester United. A year later, he moved to the Saudi Arabian team Al-Nassr.

Ronaldo kicks the ball while playing for Al-Nassr.

Ronaldo has become the highest-paid soccer player in the world. He also has a lifetime deal with Nike to endorse their products. This makes him only the third athlete to work with Nike for life. Pro basketball players Michael Jordan and LeBron James also have this high-paying contract.

CHAPTER 4

Ronaldo in 2017

AND THE WINNER IS

Who do you think is the winner of this smackdown? Everyone has their own opinions, and that's okay. Not everyone will agree. It makes being a sports fan fun!

Ronaldo has had a successful career. He has played in over 1,200 professional games and leads whatever team is lucky enough to have him as a player. In 2024, he was still playing at 39. Though he was still searching for that World Cup win, he had already scored more pro goals than Maradona.

Maradona earned an amazing World Cup win. And he shared the FIFA Player of the Century award with another soccer great, Pelé. He was beloved in Argentina and Italy for his amazing skills on the field. Maradona retired from playing soccer on his 37th birthday.

Maradona (left) plays for Argentina.

Maradona runs with the ball during the 1986 World Cup.

With their different styles of play, Maradona and Ronaldo are unique players. But Ronaldo wins this smackdown because he has been one of the best players in the world for more than two decades. As of 2024, he has no plans to retire. Who would you choose?

Ronaldo (right) plays for Al-Nassr in 2023.

SMACKDOWN BREAKDOWN

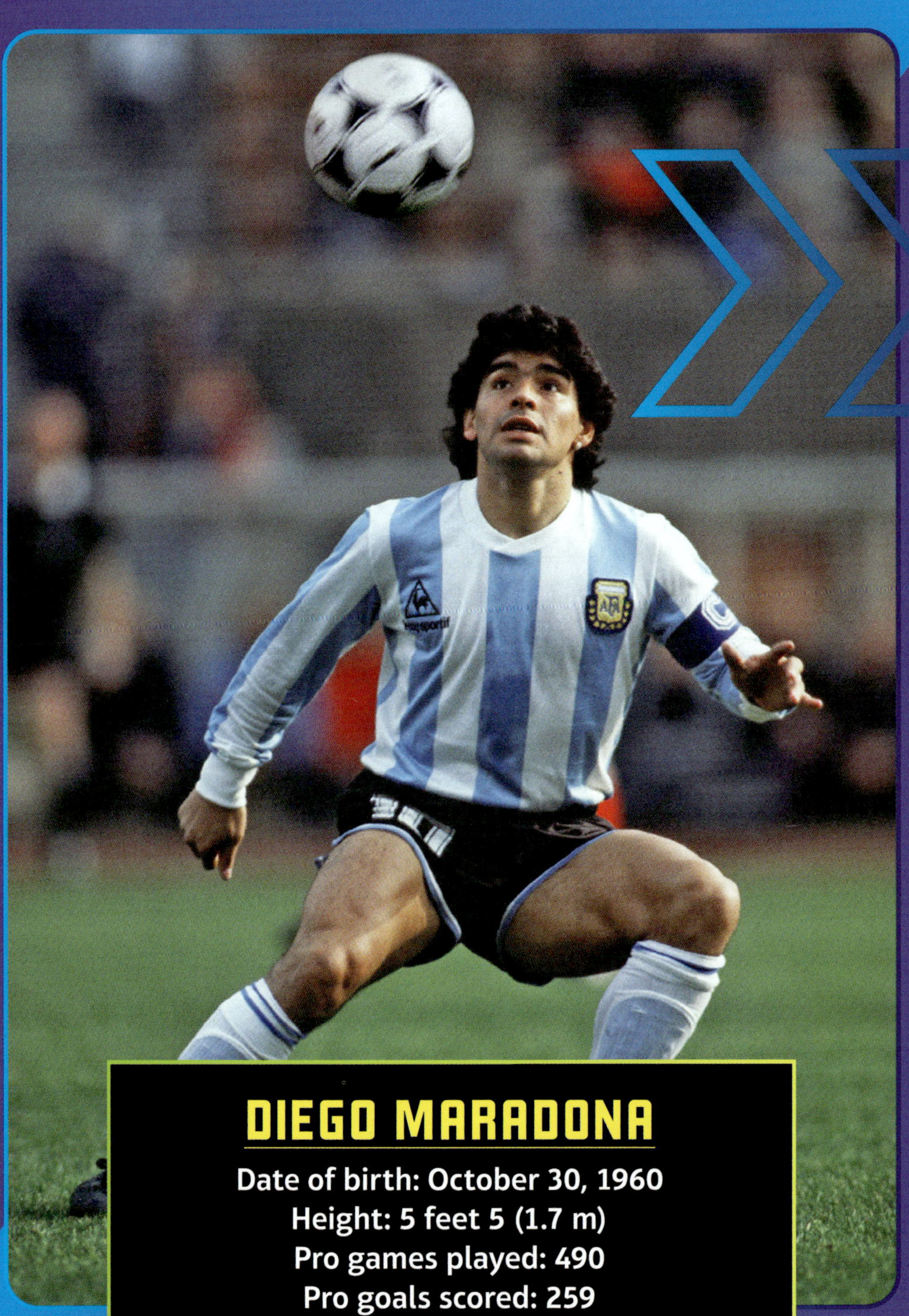

DIEGO MARADONA

Date of birth: October 30, 1960
Height: 5 feet 5 (1.7 m)
Pro games played: 490
Pro goals scored: 259
World Cup wins: 1

Stats are accurate through 2023.

CRISTIANO RONALDO

Date of birth: February 5, 1985
Height: 6 feet 1 (1.9 m)
Pro games played: 1,200
Pro goals scored: 868
World Cup wins: 0

GLOSSARY

assist: a pass that leads to a goal by a teammate

endorse: to get paid to recommend a person or product

FIFA: the group that oversees international soccer

forward: a soccer player whose main job is to score goals

Golden Ball: an award given to the best player at a World Cup

junior team: a pro or national team that is not the top team

ovation: enthusiastic applause

pitch: a soccer playing field

semifinal: a game or a series of games coming before the final round in a tournament

senior team: a top pro or national team

title: a championship

LEARN MORE

Britannica Kids: Cristiano Ronaldo
https://kids.britannica.com/students/article/Cristiano-Ronaldo/544883

Britannica Kids: Diego Maradona
https://kids.britannica.com/students/article/Diego-Maradona/490102

Buckley, James, Jr. *Who Is Cristiano Ronaldo?* New York: Penguin Workshop, 2022.

Kiddle: Football (Soccer) Facts for Kids
https://kids.kiddle.co/Football

Leed, Percy. *Pro Soccer by the Numbers*. Minneapolis: Lerner Publications, 2025.

Stabler, David. *Meet Cristiano Ronaldo*. Minneapolis: Lerner Publications, 2023.

INDEX

PHOTO ACKNOWLEDGMENTS

Image credits: Getty Images, pp. 4, 21; AP Photo/Cal Sport Media, p. 5; AP Photo/David Klein/Sportimage/Cal Sport Media, p. 6; AP Photo/picture-alliance/dpa, pp. 7, 26; AP Photo/Tsugufumi Matsumoto, p. 8; AP Photo/Eduardo Di Baia, p. 9; JOEL ROBINE/Getty Images, p. 10; Eamonn McCabe/Popperfoto/Getty Images, p. 11; AP Photo/Press Association, p. 12; AP Photo/Martin Rickett, p. 13; PA Images/Alamy, pp. 14, 25; AP Photo/Massimo Sambucetti, p. 15; Aflo Co. Ltd./Alamy, p. 16; WENN US/Alamy, p. 17; AP Photo/Manu Fernandez, p. 18; AP Photo/Thibault Camus, p. 19; AP Photo/Kreifelts, p. 20; AP Photo/Jonathan Moscrop/ZUMA Wire/Cal Sport Media, p. 22; Power Sport Images Ltd/Alamy, pp. 23, 27; AP Photo/Jack Abuin/ZUMA Wire/Cal Sport Media, p. 24; Allstar Picture Library Ltd/Alamy, p. 28; AP Photo/Martin Rickett/PA Wire, p. 29.

Cover: Allstar Picture Library Ltd/Alamy; AP Photo/Frank Hoermann/SVEN SIMON/picture-alliance/dpa.